This book intends to roundly praise
the ways that dogs enrich our days,
and show how dogs are worthy of
our admiration, thanks, and love.

To learn more about illustrator Marie Helinski and writer Jeffrey Zygmont, go to the People page at freepeepub.com.

Songs of Dogs
Poems, Pictures and Stories for the Love of Dogs

Free People Publishing
Salem, NH
freepeepub.com

ISBN: 978-1-959341-04-8
Library of Congress Control Number: 2024935757

Printed in the United States of America

CONTENTS

Poems

Stories

To the Reader

Everyone who enjoys and appreciates dogs will enjoy this book. You don't have to be a fan of poetry. I take the art very seriously, but I write poetry to reach all people, fans, newcomers and casual readers alike.

When written in language and forms that all readers can grasp, poetry unites us around our shared thoughts and feelings. It expresses sentiments we feel deeply. It uncovers important ideas and inklings that the art of language makes recognizable. Therefore these reflections and observations about dogs are more powerful, and more enjoyable, *because* they're poems – especially because they're poems that aim to speak to every person.

A poem creates a feeling inside of you through sound, while it also delivers a message through the meanings of its words. That combined appeal to both heart and head gives poetry its unique power. To experience it, read the poems slowly, so you hear them. If you can't read them aloud to yourself, fully form each word in sequence in your mind, as if you're privately reciting.

The two fictional stories included here also explore and celebrate our complex and rewarding friendship with dogs, emphasizing the mystical bonds we share with them.

Marie Helinski ties all the writings together with drawings that show the wide range of behaviors our dogs display, from whimsical to studious, from restful to energetic. Like the poems printed here, Marie's drawings reach deep beneath their surface of earnest simplicity.

As a package, *Songs of Dogs* is a warm tribute to incredible animals and the people who love and admire them. Enjoy it.

Jeffrey Zygmont

FRIENDSHIP

Overloaded

All members of the canine clan possess
an overflow of random happiness,
conveyed in toothy tongue-wags when they run,
their grins expressing joy from idle fun.
And shown when dogs display through mooning eyes
affection for the people whom they prize.
And seen when dogs recline in peaceful sleep
at home with those whose company they keep.

The Dog in Full

If we attempt to catalog
the graces that describe a dog,
we will require a long delay
that stalls the progress of today,
to give ourselves the many hours
we'd need to list a canine's powers.
Instead we will abbreviate,
list only traits that dominate,
and limit talk to just a few
dog virtues that we here review.

A place to start is playfulness,
a dog's eternal youthfulness.
Its readiness to bound and run
at any age transfers the fun
to we who keep its company;
a dog exudes frivolity.

Another trait is diligence,
commitment to its group's defense.
A dog will never hesitate
to rid its chosen real-estate
of rude intruders who intend
some harms the dog will apprehend.

Composure is an attribute
that's worthy of our pert salute.
Oh yes, a dog's excitable.
But when it rests, it rests in full.
The dog attains complete repose,
and pleads we also deeply doze.

Now to conclude, we mention love,
the gift a dog displays above
all other virtues constantly,
which we return abundantly.
With love enshrined upon its top,
our list is rich and here can stop.

My Companion

The hiking trail makes really just
a moderate incline

still low upon its rise to Garfield Ridge.

And graciously it switches back to
stepping stones or bridge

to cross a falling brook from time to time.

My bounding dog stays steady and endures
the summer's heat

as we proceed together on the path,

but separates and plunges to enjoy a
cooling bath

at junctures where the trail and water meet.

I wait upon her wading with such
soothing luxury

and grin to watch her slake her drooling thirst.

She earns these opportunities to take
her pleasure first

as payment for her joy attending me.

Chain of Command

This droll patrol my dog and I make daily
is just an antic act when we pretend
that my end of the leash controls us wholly,
the dog meanwhile stays on the servile end.

But everyone who walks a dog agrees
the strolling order really is reversed.
The dog is free to saunter where it please;
the human follows, hopelessly coerced.

Nourishment

A dog is a stomach, and my dog is that,
hounding me nightly when supper is near,
ravenous when I make supper appear,
slavering over the rich and the fat,
spilling wet morsels out onto her mat,
licking her bowl when her feeding spree ends,
strolling away as her stomach distends,
slumbering sated, impassive and flat.

But gluttony isn't her highest achievement.
Friendship is what she does best,
rambling eagerly, seeking no rest,
matching my stamina without relent,
happy where my curiosity sent
together the two of us off to explore,
walking beside me and wanting no more,
returning home gratefully, finally spent.

Her primary aim is to brighten my mood.
I show her I'm grateful by bringing her food.

Home's Odor

My dog emits a unique winter stink,
which I attribute to his sweating paws,
whose under-pads are black, but one is pink,
and follow canine perspiration laws.
Which state the only place a dog can sweat
is underneath its feet, to leave a scent
to sniff when it strays far, thereby to get
a guide to lead it back from where it went
and so return to home. I don't know why
the smell is strongest in the winter season,
and lingers long in rooms where he may lie,
and scents the house – whatever is the reason,
I treasure such rich whiffs reminding me
a free beast shares my home in harmony.

Unity

Her happiness upon a hiking trail
is all the satisfaction I require.
To watch her swinging tongue and swaying tail
is like attaining any grand desire.
Her eager ecstasy is unrestrained.
She puts no bounds around her joyfulness.
My dog runs with exuberance unchained.
When in the wilds her darting jumps express
a unity with nature: she is home.
And so she leaps and gambols and cavorts.
She veers from tree to stone. Her senses roam.
She finds enticing smells. She sniffs. She snorts.
And she excites the same delight in me,
when hiking while my dog is running free.

Partners

He is the finest sight that there can be.
I'm looking at my dog approaching me,
attentive, at a trot from where he paused,
to close the distance that his sniffing caused,
rejoining me where I have walked ahead,
enthused by where our wanderings have led,
content to stay beside me as we journey;
he is the finest sight that I can see.

Peace

The dog lies in her bolstered bed
as if she's in a cupping nest.
She curls her body, tucks her head,
and gives herself to total rest.
And gives me comfort, seeing her,
to see how she feels so secure,
and knows no mayhem may occur
inside this home I make for her.

Dog Sense

The dog applies its probing nose
so closely to the roadside stone,
where commonly dog urine goes
as each dog marks it as its own,
one micron separates the two.
I wonder how it gets so near.
I wonder what is coming through
to make the dog seem so sincere.
Its nostrils almost touch the stone.
They flare and close with rhythmic whiffs.
Possessed by one concern alone,
absorbed by scents it deeply sniffs,
the dog commits its total soul
to impulses occurring now.
It sees no obscure future goal,
no past remorse to fix somehow.
But I am rushed and can't allow
so many precious seconds burn.
I tug the leash. The dog must bow.
I miss the lesson I must learn.

The Guy Across the Street

My dog annoys only one neighbor of mine,
who claims that its barking is frequent and loud.
But irking that neighbor is cause to feel proud.
The neighbor himself is the neighborhood cloud.
He's brooding and angry and ugly and mean.
He's vain. He's combative. He's envious, green.
His twisted expressions and grunts are obscene.
His hostile behaviors increase and combine.
So irking this person is fitting and fine.

And anyway, nothing would placate the man.
His need to demean exceeds every desire.
It's not the dog's barking that raises his ire,
but one more excuse to spew venom and fire.
He yearns for attention, he needs to stand out.
He thinks he's entitled to neighborhood clout.
The more he feels challenged, the louder his shout
to trouble his neighbors as much as he can.
He festered before the dog's barking began.

Now how do I reconcile dog and this guy,
and weave them together in one loping poem?
The dog is the daylight, the neighbor is gloam.
The neighbor defiles, the dog brightens a home.
The mean man exhibits a truth we must heed
each time he erupts in a petulant screed,
that dogs represent the superior breed
whose bark is a guide to judge character by,
when perturbing person barks back in reply.

This Moment

I wonder what she's sniffing at.
My dog, I mean. She smells a cat,
or something else that crossed my lawn.
Her nose is low, her ears are drawn,
and all her senses concentrate
on something passing here of late.
As if all fate depended on
some trespasser who now is gone.

I wish I could so thoroughly
devote my mind to cares I see
in present time, occurring now,
ignoring whispers that allow
my thoughts to fret on former woes,
or worry where my future goes.
My dog with greater wisdom gives
herself to where the moment lives.

Visiting Scholar
(Ode to Flower)

My daughter's dog just sleeps.
As dog-sitter, I'm watching her.
She seldom even peeps.
She sprawls upon the kitchen floor
because, of course, she eats.
I fear that she might nip my hand
each time I offer treats.
And whether food is dry or canned,
or plain or mixed with meats,
the dog attacks her dinner and
it instantly depletes.

Yet when my daughter soon returns
and my dog-sitting ends,
when I am free of dog concerns
and they rejoin as friends,
I'll miss the mutt around my house
for lessons I have learned.
Although I gripe, complain and grouse,
her tenure here is earned.
A dog exists to sleep and eat
and, if not spayed, to breed.
And gaining these, she feels complete,
an outlook I should heed.

Testing the Waters

Dogs look funny drinking water,
slowly dropping nose to bowl,
touching tongue to just the surface,
careful, with composed control.

Then plunging tongue they slurp and slobber,
splashing droplets everywhere.
Makes you wonder why they bother
starting first with so much care.

Like a person who's uncertain
some reward is worth the risk –
takes a taste, then is immersed in
pleasures too rich to resist.

The Independent Mind

When I and my dog walk while she is leashed,
then I am leashed as well, one end for each.
Therefore I much prefer to let her run,
a practice that sometimes annoys someone,
who glowers at us, sometimes stops to scold.
I understand; I am not over-bold.
But I explain that when the dog walks free
the looseness liberates both her and me
to both approach the world without restraint,
advancing as we walk without the taint
of tethered steps that keep us too aligned
to common paths, and frees us both to find
new avenues that open up to each
such truths that those in groups could never reach.

Winter Rain

The snow beneath my dog's paws was compressed,
and softer snow surrounded every track,
with denser snow below where each paw pressed
in tracks where he had frolicked out and back.
But now as rainfall melts away the snow
the softer stuff is disappearing first
so that his paw imprints appear to grow
to elevated tufts, their heights reversed:
His tracks that once were staggered surface pits
now stand as dainty pillars thrust above
the melting surface that now lower sits,
impressions now embossed as emblems of
our impotence as Nature changes face
and we track paths its change will soon erase.

INSTINCT

The Dog Endures

My dog eats suet I hang for the birds
when little specks of fat fall from the feeder
and land upon the ground like random turds,
my canine finds and eats them like she's eager.
As if I don't already feed her well
with purchased food that's packed with nourishment,
which satisfies her hunger, I can tell,
and yet she grubs where birds leave excrement.
It's clear she can't deny the primal urge
to relish food wherever it is found.
It's clear domestication did not purge
survival instincts from this modern hound.
She is an animal, and I admire
her savage smolder of primordial fire.

Blind Luck

Brown rabbit, my black dog just saved your life
when he attacked and chased you from the grass,
before a graver fate could come to pass
from talons that would dice you like a knife.
The hawk was perched above you on a limb
while you sat on the lawn's edge unaware.
Contentedly you would have lingered there
until the hawk descended at its whim
and took you for a meal. Except my pet
first charged and made you flee into the woods,
the safest place among your neighborhoods.
The watching hawk departed with regret.
Thus rescued from a death you never saw,
you show how luck is part of Nature's Law.

Role Playing

Before the deer will raise its tail to flee,
it flicks it side to side uncertainly.
The tail's white underside shows partially,
prepared to signal full emergency.
The dog meanwhile stands poised and motionless.
It holds its sharp nose pointed to its prey.
Its forward muscles stretch, its rear compress,
as it prepares to launch and bound away.
Then at the instant it springs to attack,
the deer erects its tail's white underside.
Alerted, other deer nearby rear back,
and dash to find a place to safely hide.
As predator, the dog assaults from need.
The prey escape through thoughtfulness – and speed.

A Monument

My dog was such a rowdy pup,
one day she chewed a downspout up,
which drained down from a gutter above
to reach an elbow at the ground
connected to an open pipe
for spewing water all around –
three pieces placed in service of
the urgency when rains grow ripe
and streams of streaking sheets abound
to drain rain water harmlessly
from off the roof with gravity.

But mostly they wait empty.
Except as a protective cave
when little critters must escape
attacks from dogs that don't behave,
which was my dog when she was new
and pert and sometimes nasty.
She chased a small chipmunk into
the open pipe below the spout
that ran down from the gutter trough.
She grr-ed and growled and pounced about.
Intent to rout the chipmunk out,
she tried to chew the downspout off
and gnawed it to a flattened shape.

Made just from thin aluminum,
the downspout now remains deformed.
It shows the pandemonium
released when my dog's blood is warmed.
Deep scored, with punctures from her teeth,
distorted, flattened, pinched and crushed,
obstructed when rains must be flushed,
the downspout and the pipe beneath
display uncapped vitality,
a pup's relentless energy,
and Nature's avid savagery,
all traits that I enjoy to see.
I hope the chipmunk snuck away.
The crushed downspout and pipe can stay.

Security

The skunk ambles as if it awkwardly gallops,
forward legs reaching and hinter legs thrusting,
moving too slowly to be said to run,
sauntering casually, fearing no one.
I say to my dog we must leave it alone;
a skunk on the prowl keeps a trail as its own.

Natural Selection

A dog indoors demands you stay alert,
and be prepared to hustle him outside,
or you may find a turd or yellow squirt
inside the building where you both reside.
Although that goes against his inclination.
The dog prefers to keep his household clean.
He goes as last resort and feels frustration
to soil the floor and see his home demeaned.
A dog regards his home as someplace sacred,
from instincts to keep order to survive.
The virtue is genetically inbred,
since cleanliness kept ancestors alive.
Domesticated dogs require our aid
to open doors to gifts that Nature made.

Ode to an Aging Dog

Because I have so many friends
I'll cope all right when her life ends.
I'm speaking of my loyal dog,
who has been with me for so long
I know her death is creeping near,
and therefore know I must prepare
for sadness that will make me shake
because the loss will be so great
when my companion walks no more,
a day I fear and I'll abhor.

But yet that day is not yet here,
which makes my mourning premature,
which makes me wish I could escape
foreknowledge – not yet see the shape
of future hurts I must endure,
whose coming I foresee are sure.
One curse of human intellect
is knowing what we must expect,
which taints our pleasures felt today
with dread of pain still far away.

But I was speaking of my hope
that other friends will help me cope
with loss and loneliness I'll feel,
and ease me through the sad ordeal.
By *other friends* I mean the sprites,
the spirits, souls and silent wights
that I encounter with my dog

on roadsides that we walk along,
on forest trails, in mountain air,
such friends are hiding everywhere.

Together we meet patient trees
who grew to heights in slow degrees.
Wise boulders stare as we walk past.
We're waved to by tall meadow grass.
The wind salutes by showering leaves.
The moon keeps secret what she sees –
although my dog can see it too.
Thus she expands our common view
with instincts that attract her eyes
to friends I later recognize.

So yes, my fellowship depends
on objects she first greets as friends.
She's closer to the noble Earth
by virtue of her lower birth.
An animal in full, she feels
dim links my intellect conceals
beneath its overload of thought,
until by her sense I am brought
back into Nature's harmony,
joined by the link she shares with me.

My dog's affection brings me near
such loves that would be absent here
without her. Thus, when she must die,
I'll give her spirit to the sky,
while I collapse, relent and cry.

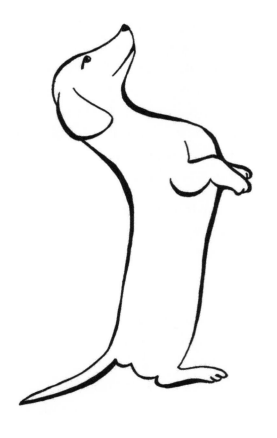

FATE

Allie and Casey's
Goodbye to Belle

She was a forlorn door-step dog
who joined us accidentally.
We rescued Belle from drear and fog
and welcomed her as family,

where she became our bouncing clown,
our playful friend who faithfully
distributed her joy around
with warmth and antic comedy.

Now as our little dog is called
to join the white eternity,
for her reward we stand resolved
to cherish her in memory.

Old Age

No self-respecting dog
can possibly ignore
the scented wild allure
of fleetly fleeing deer.

That surely means my own,
although he is so old.
He braces and grows bold
when deer pursuits unfold.

He makes an agile jog,
and dashes at the game,
while yelps and barks exclaim
he still remains the same

as every other dog,
regardless of their age;
all zestfully engage,
all gleefully rampage,

retaining youthful joy,
with tincture of the wild,
exuberant when riled,
eternally a child.

So seems my dog to me.
May we forever be.

Reward

This foam-filled bed is comforting
for both the dog and me.
The dog enjoys some cushioning
to bones grown old and aching.
For me there's satisfaction,
to see him get what he deserves.
His years of dedication
have earned the rest this bed confers.

Inevitability

I find I must walk slower now.
My dog's old age does not allow
the eager pooch to trot ahead.
She trails behind and limps instead.

And though I'm faster than the dog,
I also find our walk's a slog.
For I have aged well past my peak,
and now my legs are growing weak.

But I don't mind our slower pace.
We never aimed to rush and race.
Our aim is simply to embrace
the world encountered face to face.

Which we still manage very well.
Enthusiasms still compel
the dog and me to roam and rove
as in our younger days we strove

to follow where a trail-fork goes,
to heed the caw and call of crows,
to startle frogs and see them splash,
to chase deer – though we slowly dash.

Yet still we feel the same fast thrill.
I'll ramble with my dog until
our happy legs no longer hold.
We will expire, but not grow old.

Before Goodbye

I'm sad my dog now grows senile,
companion for so long a while.
I hate to see his senses fade,
and point toward our final trial.

With sadness I cannot evade,
my debt to time must soon be paid,
with sorrow as remittance for
those former days we romped and played.

As we consumed what each day bore,
our love accumulated more.
The dog's exuberance supplied
my guide to find the boisterous core

of happiness, which hides inside
a person, till he walks beside
a dog, since dogs expose and share
the primal joy all lives provide.

And dogs continue unaware
of time's advance, and never care
to mourn for life's approaching end.
Each present moment holds them there.

Which comforts me, to know my friend
loves all he still can comprehend.
I'm grateful I alone will bear
the sorrow poised to soon descend.

Grand Finale

Of all the changes I have seen
my dog endure, this final stage
stands as the most remarkable.
She's elderly at age sixteen,
well past a dog's expected age,
her stride no longer powerful,
her hair without a lustrous sheen,
her body bony, winnowed, weak,
with joints that click, restrict and creak,
her senses dulled to semi-keen,
her movements slow and insecure,
her mind now stymied and unsure.

But yet the essences remain:
When walking on our standard route,
I watch her dash ahead of me
with all the speed she can attain
to chase a deer I did not see,
to which her sight remains astute,
to which she can't resist pursuit.
She runs a distance in the lead,
and when her chase does not succeed
she stops. And I am well behind.
The dog then lifts her nose to find
my scent, so we be recombined.

I see the dog stand resolute:
She will not quit our standard route.
She knows I must be somewhere near.
She knows we dwell together here.
She knows we share each scent and sight.
She peers ahead, then left and right.
Her faithfulness is absolute
to creatures she considers dear.
Her essence is her constancy,
her undiluted loyalty.
And holding love within her soul,
still at this age, the dog is whole.

Where Dogs Go

A supernatural story about ever-after

This strange and satisfying episode began when I found myself occasionally noticing dogs near me. They were watching me. In each case the dog never appeared directly within my line of sight, but always in my peripheral, in a side area where my vision was indistinct. I saw each one clearly enough to recognize that the dog stood, or maybe it sat, in a state of attention as it regarded me. I saw each one clearly enough to want to turn to get a better view, to bring each mysterious mutt fully before my frontal vision. But every time I turned for a full glance, I saw no dog.

Where were they coming from? How did they get in my house? Why did that brown and black mongrel standing in the opening between my kitchen and dining room vanish when I turned to see it more clearly?

My own dog had died about two months earlier. Wilma had been medium sized, about two feet tall and very slender. She was a tight bundle of electrified muscle, and that made her difficult. She flared out of control completely, spontaneously and frequently. Inside the house she barked piercing rupp-rupps at any small disturbance. Outside the house, encountering a rival pooch, she yipped and rupped convulsively and pulled insistently against her leash. A choke collar was the only way I managed her.

Sure, I felt deep pangs of sorrow when Wilma died those two months before the phantoms arrived. But as much as I mourned her, I also felt relieved. I hadn't replaced her with a new pet, like I had all of my dogs before her. So I couldn't dismiss the mysteriously vanishing canines now appearing in my side vision as hallucinations or wishful errors because I missed my former dog.

Besides, I felt their presence too certainly to consider the visiting dogs just illusions.

The dogs came along when I went outside to clear fallen leaves, an annual Autumn ritual in this outer New England suburb. While raking, I glimpsed a pooch vaguely in my side vision. It was sitting at the end of a hedge, watching me attentively the same as the indoor dogs had watched me. Also like the indoor dogs, it vanished when I turned to view it more directly.

I resolved to turn faster next time. When my side-vision caught a yellow retriever watching me from the same spot at the end of the hedge, I spun immediately to face it. Yes, I saw it squarely within my view. The dog spun away quickly, retreating out of sight behind the hedge. I raced to the spot and scanned in the direction it ran. Yes, I saw it again, stretched into a medium stride and slipping into some low brush. I ran there rapidly, staying in close pursuit as the dog approached a street. A street! I braced instinctively and listened for the whoosh that would signal that a car was near. Naturally one came straight on trajectory and struck the dog squarely as it crossed. I saw the car's bumper and grille make impact. The vehicle drove uninterrupted through the collision. It didn't even slow. The dog had to be mutilated. I cursed the driver as I sprinted to the spot. But when I arrived, no dog.

I bent low and examined the pavement. No blood. No fur tufts. I thought, perhaps the dog hadn't been hit as dead-on-center as I had seen. Maybe the mutt had just glanced off the edge of the bumper. I scanned the area across the street. Perhaps it was limping and injured. But I saw no sign of any animal anywhere and no indication that an impact had ever occurred. And, come to think of it, I hadn't heard a thud. I'd only *seen* the strike. Or thought I had. It seemed as if the running mutt had dissolved and disappeared the instant it contacted the car.

The next time a dog appeared I launched immediately into the fastest sprint I could manage. Like before, I caught sight of the retreating canine beyond the hedge, loping toward the road like the last one. At least this time no car approached. As I raced I watched the dog safely cross the street. It stopped and curled to look back at me. This one was a Siberian husky, its eyes colored like ice.

I strained to dash faster as the dog resumed its trot. I crossed the road myself, striding hard, scarcely bothering to look for cars. The dog stopped again at a patch of forest and curled to look back at me. It seemed to be luring me, leading me. It ran into the woods. I crunched through dried fallen leaves as I entered the trees in pursuit.

From the woods I entered a large open tract that spanned about forty acres. I knew the place well because I had walked there often with Wilma, where she would scramble and ramble excitedly when let off her leash. The dog and I routinely circled a five-acre pond in the clearing and walked through a meadow that in summertime overbrimmed with tall grasses and sparkling wild flowers. The clearing was somewhat hidden, hemmed in by the woods and by a big reedy marsh that surrounded two sides. The only way to reach the secluded tract was by a narrow dirt lane that led in from a nearby street, or by crashing on foot through the woods – the way I was entering it now.

The place had changed a great deal since my last visit with Wilma two months ago. The land was raped. The ground now seemed to smolder where big machines had left wheel ruts and scraped away the grasses and flowering weeds and low-growing shrubs that had colored the place. Broken stubble and shredded woody stems stuck above the churned dirt. The area had become a depot for a construction company. A dump truck and dozer and backhoe were parked askew near an edge of the big reedy swamp. An office trailer was skewed near them. More construction gear and machines were scattered in clusters. A large load of stony dirt, the slag from a cellar excavation somewhere, made a tall naked mound.

But my focus remained on the icy-eyed husky. It had flung itself into a manic sprint, charging around the pond that lay in the clearing. It raced toward the far end of the pond, where three other dogs waited.

They waited anxiously. The three dogs spun and scurried and sniffed. They stabbed their noses at shaggy shrubs and they paced around dried autumn grasses. But none of the three dogs strayed. They behaved like they were confined, although I saw no fence or barrier.

I glanced back along the pond's shore to find the running husky. The dog had vanished.

The three canines on the pond's opposite bank still pawed and sniffed inside their hemmed space. The most energetic member of the group was a slender black dog with brown markings and a white blaze low on its throat, just like my former pet Wilma. It also behaved like Wilma: attentive, elated, over-stimulated.

I strode toward them, but stopped abruptly when a voice cut in from close beside me. "You won't be able to get to them," said a man who leaned against a rust-splotched snowplow blade detached from a truck. He was so close to me, how had I not seen him sooner?

"You can't get to them," he repeated.

I knew the guy. I had often seen him walking in my neighborhood, usually when I was walking with Wilma. We had never spoken. He had always seemed so self-absorbed and preoccupied, walking with quick, short strides, forward bent with his eyes focused down where he stepped.

"I can get there," I said. "I used to walk around that pond every day with my dog. She looked just like one of those across the water."

The man gazed at the dogs on the far shore. He watched them a moment and said, "You can't get to them now. It's different for them."

"What's different? I can see that whoever owns this place now really made a mess of it. Just in the last two months. But I don't see any fences."

"But the dogs are different now," said the man. "They'll disappear when you get close. It's like they're in a different place, even though you can see them from here."

I looked at him closely. He was short, slim and elderly, small, gray and wiry. He wore the same clothes he had worn every

51

time I'd seen him walking. They were old. They were dusty.

"How did you get here?" I asked him. "I didn't see you when I came in. Did you walk up the long driveway?"

"I came a different way," he said.

"What way?" I asked. "The only other way is to come through the woods. That's how I got in. I was chasing a dog."

"I know," he said.

"Well, I'm going over there," I said. "One of those dogs looks exactly like mine. But mine's gone. She died a couple of months ago."

"You mean Wilma," he said.

I stopped and turned squarely to face him.

"How do you know her name?" I quizzed. "Did you hear me say it out walking on the road?"

"No. It's the sort of thing I just know."

"All those times we passed on the road, you never said a word to us then."

"I know."

"Why are you talking to me now?"

"It's kind of my job. I'm here to explain."

"Explain what?"

"What do you see over there?" he asked me.

"I see three dogs, and one of them looks like my dog that just died?"

"Exactly."

"E*xactly* what?"

"That *is* your dog. That's Wilma," he said.

"That's ridiculous," I exclaimed, and began to stride again toward the pond for a closer look.

"Hold on," he said. "I'm trying to explain. Look at her for a minute. How could that dog be anyone but Wilma?"

He was right.

I whistled the single sharp blast I had used to call the dog whenever she wandered from me.

"If that was Wilma she'd be running to me right now," I said.

"But look at her," he said. "Look at them all. Do they look like they can get out of there?"

"It looks like they're in a pen," I replied.

"That's kinda what it's like for them," he answered. "It's hard to explain. But, here, let me show you something."

He led me toward the truck and dozer and backhoe parked askew near the edge of the swamp, walking with his familiar forward lean, his legs pushing out in bursts. I hustled to keep up with him.

He stopped abruptly beyond the big machines and looked down at the ground. Two deer carcasses lay amid trampled cattail reeds where the soil muddied at the marsh edge. One was a doe. The other was a buck, its antlers removed. Both were skinned, their hides removed except on their heads and the low bony portions of their legs. In places their exposed muscle bundles had begun to rot, although overall the bodies looked fresh. Hunting season had just ended, and I figured that the two deer had been shot, skinned, and dumped here just recently.

"Those are deer," I said.

"They used to be," the man corrected.

"Who threw them here?" I asked, keeping a step back.

"Probably the land's new owner."

"That's disgusting," I said.

"It's more than that," the man said. "It's an offense. We call it an impurity. It taints this whole area. That's why those dogs are stuck."

"The three dogs at the top of the pond? And the one that you say is my Wilma?"

"That's right. This is what has them caged in like that. It's hard to explain."

"I'll say," I agreed.

"After they die and get free at first they just run around," the man said. "They stay in their neighborhoods, in the places they know. They just run and run. They love it."

"Who's *they*?" I asked, fully puzzled.

"It's they. Them. Like those dogs across the pond. Like Wilma."

"You mean they're spirits?"

"You could call them that. But they're dogs. They run and run. They explore."

I thought of Wilma's unrestrained enthusiasm whenever she ran off-leash.

"But after they've run around a while they have to pass through," said the small dusty man. "They have to pass through so they can keep on running. So they never have to stop."

"Forever, you mean?"

"But only if they get through. They have to find the right place, like the pond over there."

"That's why Wilma is there?"

"Because she was so happy when she walked with you here. In this whole area here. Those two other dogs too. They loved it here too."

"Then why does it look like they're fenced in?" I asked.

"Because they are. They couldn't get through. They found this place just fine. They knew this was the place for them, the place they loved that would let them break through and run forever. But they couldn't do it because it's not like it was here before. Not when they were alive. It's defiled now. There's this impurity here."

He looked down at the skinned deer carcasses, slimy with low glisten from the onset of rot.

"There was no care here," said the man. "These two were dishonored."

"But these deer are way over here," I protested. "They're next to the swamp, not the pond."

"It's not just the pond," the man answered. "It's this whole big area here. Where the meadow was too. This whole area was their place to get through to keep running and playing. Like a big window they could go through. But now it's defiled so they're stuck. And they're running out of time. The longer they're here the smaller their area gets. It's like the window is closing. That's why they're stuck up there at the top of the pond. It's like they're in a pen that's getting smaller and smaller."

"You mean they were running around this whole clearing before?"

"But now that's the only space they have left, because by now their window is almost closed," he explained. "They've been here too long now without passing through. Their place is defiled. And now their time is running out. The space they have to break through is shrinking. It's closing in. Like a window closing."

"What happens when it closes all the way?" I asked him.

The man just shrugged, looking down grimly at the two deer carcasses.

"This impurity has to be cleaned up soon," he said. "Before their time is up and their window closes all the way.

Before they lose their chance."

"But who has to clean it up?" I asked him.

The little guy shrugged.

"Am I supposed to do it?" I wondered.

"I don't think it matters who does it," he said. "It just has to be done. These deer just need some care. I don't think it matters who does the caring."

"But what can I do?" I queried.

He shrugged. "I guess they could be buried."

"But how can I bury them here?" I questioned.

"No one else is going to do it," said the dusty wanderer. "That's why we led you here."

"Who led me here? You mean all the disappearing dogs I've been seeing . . .?"

"They were messengers. And guides," he said. "They've been trying to lead you out here. To show you."

I looked at the construction company's backhoe parked idly near us. I looked down at the deer carcasses. I gazed out across the pond at the three dogs hemmed by their closing opportunity. The bounding and boisterous mutt undeniably was Wilma.

"I bet the guy who owns all this equipment can bury the deer," I said.

🐾 🐾 🐾 🐾

Back home, I waited till around suppertime, the time when a construction crew would likely return to its depot. I drove my car to the rutted dirt lane that led into the place. The car jounced in protest as it left the pavement and entered.

I saw a parked pickup truck next to the office trailer. A man climbed out and leered at me suspiciously as I exited my own car.

"I came about those two deer," I said nervously. "It looks like somebody took the skin but didn't bury the bodies."

His expression shifted from suspicion to belligerence. He said, "Who in the eff are you?"

"I'm a neighbor. I live just over there. I came to ask if somebody can use that backhoe to bury the deer."

"What the eff are you talking about?" said the man scowling. He was large, with a big, stolid frame supporting a roundly protruding gut. "I own this effing place," he said. "You're trespassing. Get the eff out of here."

"I just came to see somebody about the deer," I repeated. "It would be easy to bury them with your backhoe."

"They're effing dead deer," he said dismissively. "They're way the eff over there."

"But they're just lying there," I persisted. "They should be treated better."

"You're a effing asshole," he said.

"Did you see those three dogs?" I tried.

"What dogs?" he said. "There aren't any effing dogs anywhere around this effing place."

I couldn't very well explain what I didn't understand myself. And his manner made me see urgently that I needed to leave his property. 🐾 🐾 🐾 🐾

I telephoned the town police. I figured that openly discarding two deer carcasses had to be some sort of violation. Maybe the local cops could insist on proper disposal. A policeman on the phone transferred me to the department's animal-control officer. The animal-control officer said that for complaints involving wild game I needed to contact the state's conservation department.

Phoning the state agency, I found my way to a conservation officer who asked a lot of specific questions that I couldn't answer. Did I know where the deer had been shot? Did I know when? Or by whom? Had they been legally harvested? Illegally? I didn't know.

He explained that I didn't have any evidence he could act on. He couldn't say if the animals had been harvested illegally if he didn't know who had killed them, and where. He couldn't know who had dumped the carcasses if many people had access to the site.

"But isn't it a terrible thing to do?" I complained. "Shouldn't they be treated better than that? Better than just being dumped near a swamp?"

"Well, yes and no," said the officer. "I mean, it *looks* bad. But you'd be amazed how many animals a full-size carcass like that will feed."

"Carcass*es*," I said. "There's two."

"Right," he continued. "You'd be amazed at how many animals will feed off of those. Especially now with Winter coming, when the snow and the cold slow down the rot. Next spring there'll be nothing left but some bones. Really. I've seen it before. Everything will feed on them, from mice on up. And all kinds of birds. Crows. Everything. And come spring, you won't see anything at all except bones."

"You mean it's a good way to get rid of the bodies?" I asked him.

"It's good for the food chain," he said. "If there's no other way to dispose of them. Of course, you wouldn't want to do it in a back yard. But if it's somewhere remote, somewhere where other animals can get to them, they'll keep a lot of animals alive through the winter."

"So you think it's a good thing? You think they were left there to feed other animals?" I asked him.

"Probably not. Probably somebody was just lazy and disrespectful and didn't want to save the meat. So they just dumped them somewhere out of the way. If I was leaving a carcass as food, I'd cut it up and scatter it a little, spread it out so more animals could get to it. So there wouldn't be as much competition between them. You know, cut off the legs and scatter them around. But either way, those carcasses are going to feed a lot of animals."

"You mean that cutting them up and scattering them would be more respectful?" I asked.

"It would show that you're leaving them for food, and not just doing something disgusting."

I purchased a one-piece hazmat suit. I purchased durable rubber gloves. I bought a respirator mask that fit over nose and mouth. I selected the most expensive knife in my kitchen, a stainless slicer with a seven-inch blade made by Wüsthof. I packed everything into a brown paper grocery bag that tucked under my arm.

"I'm recycling," I said in a stab at grim humor.

I walked through the woods along the same route the phantom husky had led me. Reaching the ravaged, newly made equipment depot, I saw the three dogs beyond the pond still sniffing and spinning and pacing anxiously as if they were penned. But their enclosure was smaller. I cut away and strode to where the two deer carcasses laid.

With the hazmat suit securely zipped and covering me neck to toes, with its hood snugged over my head, with the respirator mask shielding my nose and mouth and the thick rubber gloves pulled high on my wrists, I knelt beside the first carcass and went to work. The muscle fibers were tough. They were putrid. The meat glistened with slime and with white frothy growths of bacteria. Goo coated my gloves. Jellied meat bits clung to the knife. I grunted. I pushed the knife through to a bone. Probing, I couldn't find the shoulder joint. I grunted and tried a higher cut. The knife stopped again against bone. When I finally found the joint, I worked the knife down deeply enough to wedge its point between bones. The shoulder stayed stubbornly together. My Wüsthof was plainly outmatched. But I stayed at the task.

I was close to removing a leg when a pickup truck arrived. It rolled toward some equipment at a distant part of the site. It stopped. It turned. It trundled toward me. The burly property owner climbed out. Two other men climbed out of the truck's other side, like spectators craning for a closer view.

Standing over me where I knelt at the mutilated deer, the owner said, "You're that effing asshole that was here yesterday, aren't you? You look like an effing idiot."

I looked up at him and spoke through the mask. I didn't know what to say. I muttered about dismembering the deer so I could scatter their parts.

"What?" he said.

I repeated it. The mask muffled my voice.

"What in the eff are you talking about," he said.

I pulled the respirator mask below my chin. My glove smeared it with gooey blots from the rancid meat. I tilted my head upward to keep my chin from touching it.

"I'm cutting them apart so I can scatter their legs a little," I said. "That makes it easier for more animals to eat them. It's a more respectful way to treat the bodies."

I turned back to the task. Silently I braced for the man to seize me or push me or strike me.

After watching for a moment he said, "You never did this before, did you?"

"No."

"There's better tools you could use," he said. "That knife's no good for this."

"It's all I had," I told him.

"If I help it will go a lot faster," he said. "I know how to do it. But I can't help you right now. We gotta get back to a job. We just ran back here to pick up that truck over there."

I stayed at the vile task silently.

"We'll be back around five," he said.

I thought of the dogs, the phantom dogs penned at the far end of the pond. I thought of Wilma. I thought of the strange old guy and the closing window, the passing opportunity, Wilma's time running out.

I looked up at the property owner. I said, "I'm this far. I might as well just keep going till I'm done."

Before he climbed back into the pickup he said, "They're road kill we found. It seemed better to bring them back here than just leave them there on the side of the road. I took the hides and the antlers because I can use those. But the meat was no good." Inside the truck, through the open window, he said, "I never thought of cutting them up so more animals can get to them. It's a good idea."

Alone again, I completed the butchering. The task I had guessed would take ten or twelve minutes ended up consuming more than an hour. After I dropped the last severed leg a little distance from the carcasses, my body convulsed in a long shudder, both revulsion and relief.

I walked to get a clear view of the pond where the dogs had been penned. They were there, but no longer restricted. The three pooches raced joyously and spun in a wider circumference, widening and widening as each dog pushed outward and bounded and leaped and spun again in uncontained excitement. Pushing out farthest, scampering with the greatest vigor, was the specter of Wilma.

Reflexively I whistled the long, single blast that once had called her to me. Recognizing it, she reared to stillness for an instant. With a powerful push she stretched into a sprint. She tore along the water shore, skirting the pond and charging toward me. She came at me head on, stretched low as she dashed elatedly with her snout thrust far to the fore, her jaw hinged in a pink lippy grin. I stepped one leg backward to brace for her impact. I stiffened. Wilma hurtled toward me at startling speed. This was the youthful Wilma, the dog I had known years earlier for her irrepressible energy, her constant vigor, her unrestrained elation. She reached me like a skimming torpedo, low and outstretched and sprinting maniacally, blurred from speed. She launched. She leaped higher than I ever had witnessed before, a reckless projectile striking my shoulders and chest. Instinctively I reared backward. But at the instant of impact Wilma was gone. Bewildered, I looked behind and above me to where her momentum would have carried her. No dog.

Into the air to Wilma I said, "Run fast and run hard. You're the finest friend a man can have."

I was slow to remove the streaked and gore-specked hazmat suit, slow to bundle it together with the gloves and

62

spoiled respirator and the knife, slow to roll them together inside of the brown paper grocery bag, slow to tuck the bundle under my arm and depart, consuming time until my weeping stopped.

"I miss you, crazy dog," I said as I left the spot. Instead of cutting back through the woods, the way I had come, I walked out along the rutted dirt lane that led to the road. The distance to my house along the paved and public roads was only about a half mile. Wilma and I had walked that route so many times when returning from our strolls around the pond and through the bright meadow, I walked it today in tribute to her.

A short distance from the lane and just getting started on the paved road toward home, I encountered the small old man again, walking toward me on the other side of the street with his usual private intensity, forward-bent and downward cast, self-absorbed, all of his attention on the pavement where his feet fell. When we were abreast on the two sides of the street I called out to him, "The dogs are all free now."

"I know," he said, stopping at last and turning to face me across the road.

"I'm ready to get another one now," I told him.

"You'll get another good one," said the dusty man, stepping back into his self-absorbed stride.

63

Being Versed in Country Things

Dog and child follow Nature's trail

The child and dog were inseparable that summer. Their silent bond seemed tightest the frequent times they walked together through the unsettled, unused open fields and forests that stretched behind their family's home.

The young girl loved the meadows and shaggy scrubland and patches of forest. She took them to be wild, isolated places. Though in truth the land had been used and re-used many times – for farming – for woodlots back when people cut trees for firewood to cook and heat their homes – for disposal heaps to dump bottles and trash, the heaps now long buried by overgrowth, and by the insidiously rising soil that in time covers all human works. Walking with the dog, the child saw only Nature there, abundant and undisturbed. And in fact, Nature did own the fields and forests that she loved, because it was reclaiming and regenerating them, as Nature does.

The dog loved the girl. He loved her for her gentle kindness when she sat for long moments to slowly stroke the dog's head. He loved her for her tolerance when he nudged her for attention and she patted him, never pushing the dog away. The dog loved the girl for her patience when she stood for extended spans to allow him to sniff at interesting scents when she walked him outside to "go", when instructed by a parent.

The dog especially loved the child for their long rambles on the indistinct paths through the woods and fields behind their house. He sensed the girl's reverence for the natural places. He shared her enthusiasm for always pushing out farther on their walks, her dreamy willingness to wander and her awe for small discoveries. The dog recognized the young girl's reluctance to end a ramble and return.

She never brought along a leash. The dog never strayed unreasonably far. Because of his bond with her, the dog always remained aware of the girl's location, even when the dog and she were out of each others sight, even though the girl was moving along a path.

A clear sunlit morning, the girl startled at a squeal or loud squeak or high screech from a shrubby scrub patch where the dog had disappeared. She raced toward the blaring alarm. The dog clenched a small rabbit in its teeth. The squealing creature was no larger than her two hands knit together. The girl skidded onto her knees when she reached them. She grasped the dog's snout and jaw and pulled them apart and turned his head downward so that the captured rabbit fell to the ground. As she pulled away the dog by his collar, she noticed a crimson jewel of blood dotting the baby rabbit's brown fur.

At supper that evening she asked her father, "What kind of voices do rabbits have?"

"Wild rabbits?" he quizzed. "Usually they're quiet and you don't hear any sound at all. But I've seen some caught by cats that scream so loud that they scare you."

"He caught a baby one today," the girl said as she looked at the dog on the floor. "Do you think it's still alive?"

"Was it screaming," he asked her.

"It was real loud."

"If it was screaming loudly, it probably was hurt pretty bad," her father explained.

As the week passed her sadness and regret over the incident faded. She still sometimes pictured the small rabbit's soft fur with the upwell of red at the puncture site. But the memory's sharpness diminished.

An afternoon with the sun hot and nearly vertical overhead, the girl and the dog walked on a faded, dusty track that ran along a woodline on one side, with a mowing field on the other. The field was one of the last that a farmer in the town worked, mowing the meadow grass to make hay to feed to his lolling handful of cattle. The field had just been mowed. She saw no sign of the old farmer's puttering tractor or the cutter bar champing behind it. But the field's tall grass was shorn to stubble and lay on the ground.

The dog trotted onto the leveled mowing field while the girl stayed on the lane, mostly disregarding the dog, absorbing summer's pleasantness.

But she shuddered when she realized that the dog, after veering onto the field, now was creeping with stealth toward a spot that keenly drew its focus. The image of the captured small rabbit rushed into her inner vision. Was he stalking another wild animal? She hollered the dog's name and dashed toward it into the field.

She caught the dog just steps before he reached an exposed bird's nest on the ground. With her hand cinched firmly under and around the dog's collar, she dragged him away. As she tugged against his protests, she glanced and saw clearly the woven assembly of fine stems and twigs that made up the nest. With the meadow grass that had hidden the nest and sheltered it and shaded it from harsh sunlight now cut and lying flat on the ground, she plainly saw the three scrawny chicks that stood up in the nest and stretched their necks upward and waggled their heads and pink bodies in confusion.

The girl kept firm hold of the collar and ran beside the dog, guiding it, as they retreated back along the dirt lane toward home. She released him only after she felt certain the dog had grown distracted enough to forget the exposed nest.

"Mom," she called loudly as she banged in through the back door, making sure the dog scrambled inside beside her. "Mom," she said, "we found a nest of baby birds out there on the ground. The farmer cut down all the tall grass and now the nest is right out in the open."

"They're probably Bobolinks," her mother said. "They like to make nests on the ground. They know how to make them safe and hidden."

"But, mom, it's not hidden anymore," the girl said. "It's right out in the open."

"Nature takes care of those things," her mother replied.

"But, mom, it's so hot outside today. The birds are so little that they just have skin. They don't even have any feathers yet. I want to go back there and carry them into the shade."

Her mother regarded her for a moment, feeling tenderness.

"But, honey," said the woman, "if you move the birds the parents might not find them to bring them food. Or they might be too afraid because humans have been near."

"Then I'll build a little screen for them," the girl reasoned.

"A screen?"

68

"Yeah. I can use the cut grass and stand some up and make like little walls around them for shade. It's real long grass."

More tenderness came.

"You know you always have to be careful when you're out there," the mother said.

The girl looked toward the dog, who now slavered loudly at his water bowl on the floor.

"He can't come," the girl said.

"What do you mean?"

"He'll kill them, mom. Like he did the baby rabbit. He doesn't know any better."

"But, honey," said her mother, "I won't let you go out there by yourself."

When mother and daughter left the house they closed even the wooden inner door that normally stayed open in summer to let air enter through the outer screen door. Even with both doors firmly shut, they heard the dog inside the house barking loudly and frantically. They heard dull thuds and scrapes as the dog jumped up and clawed at the door in its eagerness to burst out and join them.

"He's going to leave marks," the mother said to the air.

In the field the three naked chicks stood up when the mother and daughter knelt beside the nest, as if the birds, hungry, were fooled about their own parents' return. At first the two humans, child and adult, struggled to make the cut long meadow grass stand again. But eventually the mother fashioned a way to make it stay, even against the breeze. Together the two of them built the screen, and gave the birds back their shade.

"Do you think it will stay, mom?" the little girl asked.

"I don't know. I hope so."

"Do you think they'll be okay?" the girl asked.

"I hope so. We've done everything we can. The rest is up to Nature."

The next morning passed as a typical child's summer morning for the girl: Rising when early sunshine pushed like a glow of lighted gold from behind her window curtain; asking for more butter on the toast her mother made her for breakfast; daring to ask if she could use her mother's phone, and shrugging in acceptance when denied use of the little screen. By nearly noon the summer day's long lassitude drove the young girl outside to let her vacantly wandering mind expand in the welcoming home Nature made, to the paths wending through the wooded acres, the fields and the stands of low scrub that stretched invitingly behind her family's home.

The dog kept to his usual pattern, staying aware of the girl as he veered away and vanished to trace scents, re-emerging sometimes ahead of the girl as she walked on the trail, sometimes behind her, then racing exuberantly to catch her, brushing her leg as he passed her to seize the lead. She stayed on a lane that ran between woods and low growth until it ended at a tee, then turned on the connecting path toward a large tree where recently an enormous bird had surprised her. She hadn't seen the bird on that day. She was unaware of it. But when the huge creature launched into flight from a limb the girl walked beneath, its great wings created gusts that shuddered palpably above her. She heard and seemed even to feel the deep movement of displaced air overhead. Startled, she had looked up only in time to see the big creature recede to the distance above the tree crowns.

Had it been an eagle, a large hawk, a great owl? She didn't know. But she regarded as sacred the site at which it first had perched and pushed its audible wind down upon her. She walked now to visit the place.

Two more days passed the same, with the girl and the dog wandering the natural tracts at their whim. On the fourth day after she and her mom had built the baby birds' enclosure, again near noon with the sun almost vertical above her, the girl realized with a start that she was walking on the faded lane alongside the mowing field. Her first impulse was to fish at the dog's neck for his collar and tug him away and retreat from the place. But the field was much changed today. The deep grass that had been cut and lay leveled and flat four days ago had since been raked into windrows to dry by the farmer on his puttering tractor, and then baled, the bales loaded onto a creaking flat wagon and towed to the barn, where the hay would wait to feed the farmer's scruffy cows through winter. Now just stubble from the cut grass remained on the field.

The girl scanned for the shelter of upright stems she had made with her mother. She saw no signs of it. Her need to know overcame her concern about mischief from the dog. She turned onto the field and strode toward the area where she thought the nest had been, the dog dutifully beside her. Scanning over the ground, pacing in a grid with her eyes focused down she looked for it. Finally the dog's intense sniffing in a single small spot showed her where the nest must have been. The dog probed remnant scents of the birds' home. But the girl saw no signs of it. Only grass stubble filled the spot.

The farmer's hay rake or baling machine might have

scooped up the nest, she thought.

"I hope they got away okay," the girl said aloud.

She looked up and peered around every edge of the shorn mowing field. Far across on the other side she saw a forest. Maybe the enormous animal, the eagle or ponderous owl that had stirred silent air above her, now perched there in the distant woods, the girl thought.

She turned back toward the forlorn trail, ready to return to it to resume their walk, but glancing once more at the ground and wondering about the nest.

"We did the best we could," she said aloud. "Now it's up to Nature."

The dog looked up at her in recognition of her voice. The dog loved the girl.

(With gratitude to Robert Frost, for his poems *The Exposed Nest* and *The Need of Being Versed in Country Things*.)

72

Feline Feelings

Marie, who drew the pictures you see here,
prefers cats over dogs. We will allow
her preference, since her drawings here make clear
the difference doesn't matter anyhow.
Whichever animal she may prefer,
her drawings show she feels an equal stir.
She understands affection for a pet.
She knows the love the animal returns.
She feels the obligation and the debt
she owes the pet, which by its life it earns.
Therefore we give Marie this page to show
how dogs and cats emit an equal glow.

Milton Keynes UK
Ingram Content Group UK Ltd.
UKHW011504050524
442175UK00001B/9